Languages of the World

Vietnamese

Charlotte Guillain

Heinemann LIBRARY

Chicago, Illinois

www.capstonepub.com
Visit our website to find out more information about Heinemann-Raintree books.

To order:

☎ Phone 888-454-2279

💻 Visit www.capstonepub.com to browse our catalog and order online.

Edited by Dan Nunn and Diyan Leake
Designed by Marcus Bell
Original illustrations © Capstone Global Library Ltd 2012
Picture research by Elizabeth Alexander
Originated by Capstone Global Library Ltd
Printed and bound in China by South China Printing
  Company Ltd

15 14 13 12 11
10 9 8 7 6 5 4 3 2 1   0864

Library of Congress Cataloging-in-Publication Data
Guillain, Charlotte.
  Vietnamese / Charlotte Guillain. 1st ed.
    p. cm.—(Languages of the world)
  Text in English and Vietnamese.
  Includes bibliographical references and index.
  ISBN 978-1-4329-5839-8—ISBN 978-1-4329-5847-3 (pbk.)
  1. Vietnamese language—Textbooks for foreign speakers—
English. 2. Vietnamese language—Grammar. 3. Vietnamese
language—Spoken Vietnamese. I. Title.
  PL4373G85 2012
  495.9'2282421—dc23   2011017930

Acknowledgments
The author and publisher are grateful to the following for permission to reproduce copyright material: Alamy pp. 8 (© mediacolor's), 20 (© Ted Foxx), 24 (© David R. Frazier Photolibrary, Inc.), 26 (© Megapress); Corbis pp. 11 (© KHAM/X01568/Reuters), 22 (© Bob Krist), 23 (© Remi Benali); Getty Images pp. 21 (Noel Hendrickson/Digital Vision), 25 (Richard Heathcote); Photolibrary pp. 7 (Shalom Ormsby), 13 (Frederic Soreau), 14 (Marc Verin), 15 (Rolf Bruderer), 17 (Jochen Tack), 28 (Sean Sprague), 29 (Per-Andre Hoffmann); Shutterstock pp. 5 (© Muellek Josef), 6 (© Stephen Bures), 9 (© Luciano Mortula), 10 (© Photobank), 12 (© Photobank), 16 (© Golden Pixels LLC), 18 (© J van der Wolf), 19 (© Rafal Cichawa), 27 (© Photobank).

Cover photograph reproduced with permission of Shutterstock (© Monkey Business Images).

Every effort has been made to contact copyright holders of material reproduced in this book. Any omissions will be rectified in subsequent printings if notice is given to the publisher.

Disclaimer
All the Internet addresses (URLs) given in this book were valid at the time of going to press. However, due to the dynamic nature of the Internet, some addresses may have changed, or sites may have changed or ceased to exist since publication. While the author and publisher regret any inconvenience this may cause readers, no responsibility for any such changes can be accepted by either the author or the publisher.

Contents

Vietnamese words in this book are in italics, *like this*. You can find them all in the word bank on pages 30–31.

Vietnamese Around the World

Vietnam is a country in southeast Asia. Vietnamese is the main language of Vietnam. In Vietnamese, the country name is written as two words: *Việt Nam.*

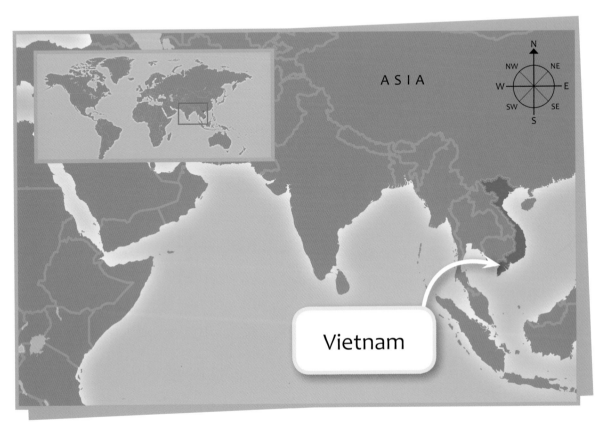

ASIA

N
NW   NE
W   E
SW   SE
S

Vietnam

How to say it
Vietnam = *Việt Nam*
Vietnamese = *tiếng Việt*
language = *tiếng*

People also speak Vietnamese in countries where Vietnamese people have gone to live. These are places such as the United States, Australia, Cambodia, and France.

Who Speaks Vietnamese?

More than 70 million people speak Vietnamese as their main language. Millions of others speak it as a second language. This means that they also speak another language at home.

Some groups of people in Vietnam speak other languages.

Vietnamese families who move abroad also speak the language of their new home country.

Over one million people in the United States speak Vietnamese. Vietnamese-Americans and Vietnamese-Australians usually only speak Vietnamese with their family and friends.

Vietnamese and French

Many Vietnamese words come from Chinese. Vietnamese used to be written in the characters used in Chinese writing.

The writing on these lanterns is in old Vietnamese.

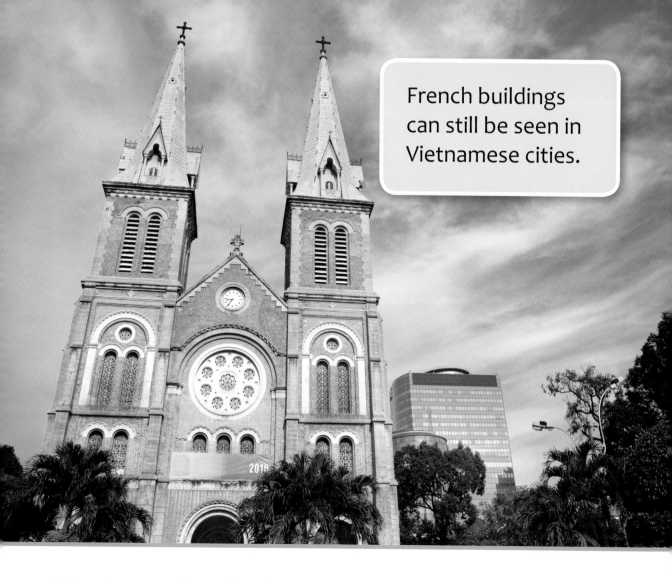

French buildings can still be seen in Vietnamese cities.

The French ruled Vietnam from the mid-1800s until the mid-1900s. People began writing Vietnamese in the Roman alphabet. This is the alphabet that is used to write French and English.

Learning Vietnamese

Vietnamese is a very difficult language to speak. The way you say a word can give it different meanings. There are different types of Vietnamese in the different regions of Vietnam.

The best way to learn Vietnamese is to listen to people speaking Vietnamese and try to copy them.

Marks called accents show small differences in the way the letters sound.

Vietnamese has some characters that are not in our alphabet. For example, the letter ô is pronounced "aw," as in "saw," and the letter ề is pronounced "ay," as in "hay."

Saying Hello and Goodbye

You can greet people in Vietnamese in different ways. When you meet for the first time, you say, "*Chào chị*" to a girl and "*Chào anh*" to a boy.

How to say it
hello = *chào chị* or *chào anh*
goodbye = *tạm biệt*

How to say it

How are you? = *Chị có khoẻ không* (to a girl)/*Anh có khoẻ không* (to a boy)

To ask someone how they are, you say, "*Chị có khoẻ không*" to a girl, or "*Anh có khoẻ không*" to a boy. To reply, you might say, "*Tôi khoẻ cám ơn,*" meaning "I'm fine, thanks."

13

Talking About Yourself

To tell someone your name, you might say, "*Tên tôi là …*" ("My name is …"). To tell them how old you are, you might say, "*Tôi là hai mươi tuổi*" ("I am ten years old").

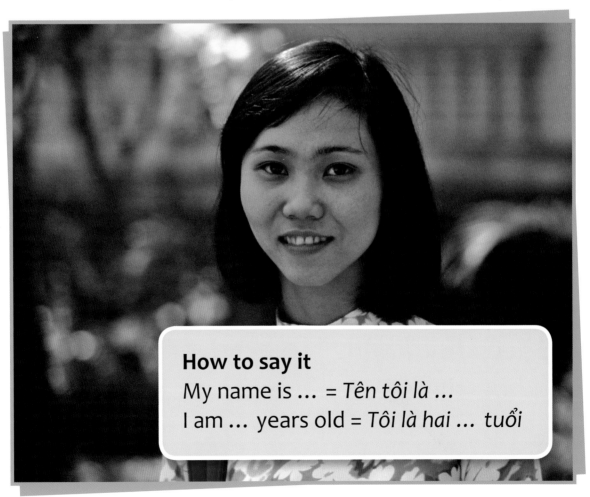

How to say it
My name is … = *Tên tôi là …*
I am … years old = *Tôi là hai … tuổi*

How to say it
I come from … = *Tôi ở …*
yes = *dạ vâng*

To tell you where they are from, someone
might say, "*Tôi ó Việt Nam.*" If someone
asks you if you speak Vietnamese, you can
say, "*Dạ vâng.*" This is a polite way to say
yes. To say no, you can say, "*Dạ không.*"

15

Asking About Others

There are different ways to say "you" in Vietnamese. It is polite to call a woman *bà* and a man *ông*. You can use *chị* for a girl and *anh* for a boy your own age.

How to say it
What is your name? = *Chị /Anh tên gi?*
How old are you? = *Bạn bao nhiêu tuổi?*

How to say it
Where do you come from? = *Chị /Anh ở đâu đến?*
Do you speak Vietnamese? = *Chị/Anh biết nổi tiếng Việt không?*

To ask where a girl is from, you say, "*Chị ở đâu đến?*" For a boy, you say, "*Anh ở đâu đến?*" To ask if a girl speaks Vietnamese, you say, "*Chị biết nói tiếng Việt không?*" or to a boy, "*Anh biết nói tiếng Việt không?*"

At Home

In Vietnam, people live in different types of homes. There are some very big, crowded cities. In the cities, many people live in large apartment buildings.

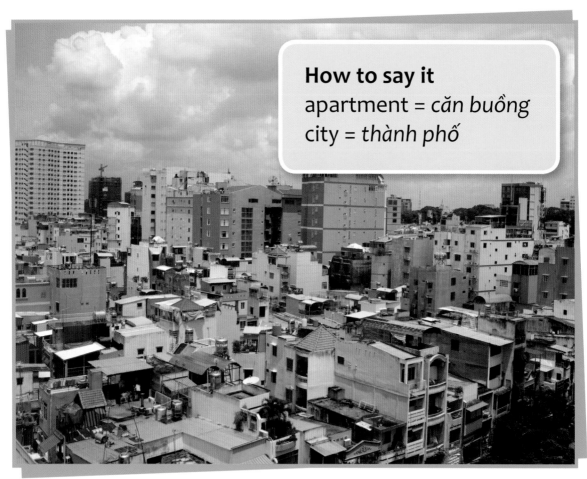

How to say it
apartment = *căn buồng*
city = *thành phố*

How to say it
house = *nhà ở*
village = *làng*

In the countryside, people live in small villages. They live in homes made from materials they can find nearby. Some homes are built on stilts, to protect them from floods.

Family Life

People often get together with uncles, aunts, cousins, and grandparents. There are different words for family members. This depends on whether they are on the mother or father's side of the family.

How to say it
family = *gia đình*
father = *cha*
mother = *mẹ*

In Vietnam, young people are expected to show respect for older people. Children care for their parents as they get older. They often live together or close by.

21

At School

In Vietnam, children start school when they are six years old. They usually wear a uniform. Sometimes children from poor families stop going to school so they can work.

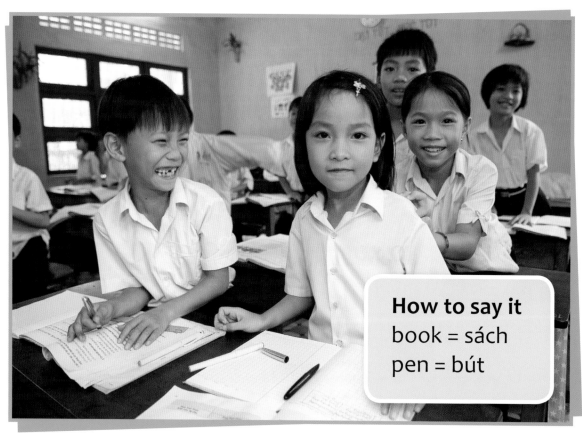

How to say it
book = sách
pen = bút

How to say it
school = *trường học*
classroom = *lớp học*
teacher = *giáo viên*

Children go to school from Monday through Saturday. At some schools, half the children go in the morning and the other half go in the afternoon.

Having Fun

People in Vietnam like doing many different things in their spare time. Many people like listening to music. In the cities, people enjoy going to the park with their families.

How to say it
park = *công viên*

How to say it
sports = *thể thao*
soccer = *quả bóng đá*

People in Vietnam like to play and watch soccer. They also play a game called sepak takraw. Players use their feet to get the ball over the net.

Food and Drink

There are Vietnamese restaurants wherever Vietnamese people have gone to live. Rice is the most important food in Vietnam.

How to say it
cooked rice = *cơm*
round rice noodles = *bún*
restaurant = *quán ăn*

How to say it
fish = *cá*
chicken = *gà*
beans = *đậu*
honey = *mật ong*
banana = *chuối*

Vietnamese cooking uses many herbs and spices. Lots of dishes include fish from rivers, lakes, and the sea. In the cities, many people enjoy eating at street stalls and open-air restaurants.

Clothes

Many people in Vietnam wear clothes like the ones you might wear, such as jeans and T-shirts. People in cities mostly dress like this.

How to say it
clothes = *quần áo*
jeans = *quần jean*

How to say it
pants = *quần cụt*
hat = *cái mũ*

Some women wear clothing called ao dai on special occasions. This is a long dress worn over pants. In the countryside, people sometimes wear traditional cone-shaped hats.

Word Bank

English	Vietnamese
ao dai (traditional Vietnamese clothing)	*áo dài*
apartment	*căn buồng*
banana	*chuối*
beans	*đậu*
book	*sách*
brother (older)	*anh*
chicken	*gà*
city	*thành phố*
classroom	*lớp học*
clothes	*quần áo*
cooked rice	*cơm*
Do you speak Vietnamese?	*Chị /Anh biết nói tiếng Việt không?*
family	*gia đình*
father	*cha*
fish	*cá*
goodbye	*tạm biệt*
grandfather	*ông*
grandmother	*bà*
hat	*cái mũ*
hello	*chào chị* (to a girl) *chào anh* (to a boy)
honey	*mat ong*
house	*nhà ở*
How are you?	*Chị có khoẻ không?* (to a girl) *Anh có khoẻ không?* (to a boy)

How old are you?	*Bạn bao nhiêu tuổi?*
I am fine, thanks	*Tôi khoẻ cám ơn*
I am … years old	*Tôi là hai … tuổi*
I come from …	*Tôi ở …*
jeans	*quần jean*
mother	*mẹ*
music	*nhạc*
My name is …	*Tên tôi là …*
no	*dạ không*
pants	*quần cụt*
park	*công viên*
pen	*bút*
restaurant	*quán ăn*
round rice noodles	*bún*
school	*trường học*
sister (older)	*chị*
soccer	*quả bóng đá*
sports	*thể thao*
teacher	*giáo viên*
village	*làng*
What is your name?	*Chị /Anh tên gì?*
Where do you come from?	*Chị /Anh ở đâu đến?*
yes	*dạ vâng*
you	*anh* (boy your age)
	chị (girl your age)
	ông (man)
	bà (woman)
younger brother, sister, or cousin of the same age	*em*

Find Out More

Books

Alberti, Theresa Jarosz. *Vietnam ABCs: A Book About the People and Places of Vietnam* (Country ABCs). Minneapolis: Picture Window, 2007.

Englar, Mary L. *Vietnam: A Question and Answer Book* (FactFinders). North Mankato, Minn.: Capstone, 2007.

Website

http://kids.nationalgeographic.com/kids/places/find/vietnam

Index